They Worked Together

Together

By Anna Prokos

Contents

Introduction   3

Edmund Hillary and Tenzing Norgay   4

Helen Keller and Anne Sullivan   10

Meriwether Lewis, William Clark
and Sacagawea   16

Conclusion   23

Index   24

Introduction

Have you ever worked in a team? Many great events in history took teamwork. This book describes three teams who worked together to reach a goal.

Edmund Hillary and Tenzing Norgay

Edmund Hillary was born in Auckland, New Zealand, in 1919. He first climbed a mountain when he was 16. After that, Edmund climbed many mountains in New Zealand and around the world.

Edmund Hillary born 1919

Tenzing Norgay was born in Nepal in 1914. Tenzing climbed many mountains around his home as he grew up. When he was older, he often helped others climb mountains, too.

Tenzing Norgay
1914–1986

China
Nepal
India
N

Mount Everest is in the Himalayan Mountain Range.

Edmund and Tenzing had the same goal. They both wanted to reach the top of Mount Everest. It is the world's tallest mountain. In 1953 Edmund and Tenzing climbed the mountain together.

Climbing Mount Everest was very dangerous.
At one point Edmund jumped across a gap in the ice
and landed on a huge block of ice. It broke away
and Edmund fell.

Tenzing held onto the rope
that tied them together. He pulled
Edmund back onto the mountain
and saved his life.

Edmund and Tenzing took seven weeks to climb Mount Everest. On 29th May 1953 they reached the top. They were the first people to reach it.

After the climb people often asked them which one had reached the top first.

"We climbed as a team," they answered.

Edmund and Tenzing continued to work together. They helped build schools and hospitals in Nepal. They wanted to give something back to the people who had helped them achieve their goal.

◀ Children welcomed Edmund at Sotang School, Nepal.

Tenzing and Edmund received medals after their climb. ▶

Helen Keller and Anne Sullivan

Helen Keller was born in Alabama,
in the United States in 1880.
When she was a baby, she got ill.
Her illness made her blind and deaf.

When Helen was five years old,
she still couldn't speak because
she couldn't hear. She needed
special help to learn.

**Helen Keller
1880–1968**

United States

Alabama

N

Then Helen's mother met Anne Sullivan and Anne was asked to teach Helen.

Anne had never been a teacher before. Still she wanted to work with Helen. Anne knew what it was like to be blind. She had lost most of her eyesight when she was a child. Anne went to a school for blind people. She wanted to help Helen go to school, too.

Anne went to a school for blind people ▼

**Anne Sullivan
1866–1936**

Anne showed Helen how to use sign language. First Anne had to sign letters in the palm of Helen's hand because Helen couldn't see. Then Helen learned to sign herself.

Helen also learned to read and write using Braille. She even learned to speak.

After a while Helen went to school with Anne. Anne listened to the teachers, then spelled their words into Helen's hand.

Helen went to school with Anne's help.

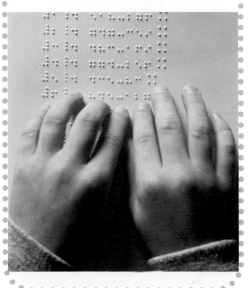

Braille

People who can't see can learn to read Braille. In Braille bumps on paper stand for letters. People use their fingertips to read the Braille.

At school Helen wrote a book about her life called *The Story of My Life*. Helen wrote many books over the years.

Helen and Anne helped other people, too. Anne showed others how to teach blind and deaf people. Helen showed blind people that they could achieve their goals. As a team they helped raise money for the blind.

Anne Sullivan and Helen Keller were admired by many people. Their lives and their work touched many people all over the world.

Children crowd around Helen during a visit to Melbourne, Australia, in 1948.

Meriwether Lewis, William Clark and Sacagawea

In 1803 people in the United States had not explored much of the land in the far western part of North America. At this time the United States only extended as far as the Rocky Mountains. People knew the Pacific Ocean was somewhere further west, but there was no route to get there.

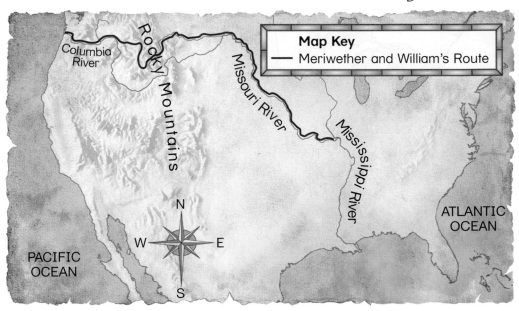

Meriwether Lewis
1774–1809

William Clark
1770–1838

President Thomas Jefferson asked Meriwether Lewis to lead a trip to explore further west. Meriwether knew many things about plants and animals. He asked William Clark to be his partner. William was a wonderful mapmaker, but the job ahead of them was difficult.

Meriwether and William needed help on their journey. They found a young Native American woman called Sacagawea (sah-KAH-gah-wee-ah). She knew about the land and could talk to the Native Americans in their own language.

Like this woman, Sacagawea probably carried her son on her back.

Sacagawea about 1786–1812

Sacagawea led the team across mountains. She found plants to eat when they ran out of food. She talked with the Native Americans they met along the way. Sacagawea also helped get horses and food when the team needed them.

Sacagawea was smart and brave.
Once her boat almost tipped over.
She quickly saved important papers
and supplies that would have been lost.
    Sacagawea saved Meriwether and
William from trouble many times.
William and Meriwether named a river
Sacagawea River to thank her for her help.

Meriwether, William and Sacagawea worked together as a team to travel across thousands of kilometres. Meriwether and William took notes and made drawings and maps. They crossed rivers and mountains. It was a long, difficult journey.

Once Meriwether was chased by a bear.

When their long trip ended in 1806, the team never forgot each other. After Sacagawea died, William took care of her son, Jean Baptiste. Meriwether, William and Sacagawea played an important part in the history of the United States and in each other's lives.

This memorial to Meriwether, William and Sacagawea is in Montana.

Conclusion

Working in a team is not always easy.
Tenzing Norgay had to save Edmund Hillary's life.
Anne Sullivan needed patience with Helen Keller.
Sacagawea had to rescue Meriwether Lewis
and William Clark many times.

What did these teams have in common?
They never gave up! Teams work hard to reach
their goals together.

Index

Alabama 10

Auckland 4

Braille 13

Clark, William 17–18,
    20–22, 23

Hillary, Edmund 4,
    6–9, 23

Jefferson, Thomas 17

Keller, Helen 10–15, 23

Lewis, Meriwether
    17–18, 20–22, 23

Mount Everest 6–8

Nepal 5, 9

Sacagawea 18–22, 23

Sacagawea River 20

Story of My Life, The 14

Sullivan, Anne 11–13,
    15, 23

Tenzing Norgay 5–9, 23